# Charts Made Simple

CALGARY PUBLIC LIBRARY

AUG     2011

to Paula,
who kept my vision clear
and made this book possible

Copyright © 2010 JC Briar
Technical editing by Karen Frisa
Indexing by Sonya Dintaman
Author photo by Marci Bacho

All rights reserved. No portion of this book may
be reproduced in any form, except for inclusion of
brief quotations in an article or review, without the
written consent of the publisher.

ISBN 978-0-9830792-0-0
LCCN: 2010915886
Printed in the US by McNaughton & Gunn
First printing: December, 2010

**Mixed Sources**
Product group from well-managed
forests and other controlled sources
www.fsc.org  Cert no. SW-COC-002283
FSC  © 1996 Forest Stewardship Council

Glass Iris Publications
PO Box 2395
Corvallis, OR 97339

To learn about other titles in the Knitting on Paper
series or to report errata, visit www.jcbriar.com.

# Charts Made Simple
understanding knitting charts visually

a Knitting on Paper book ✺ by JC Briar

Glass Iris
PUBLICATIONS

# Contents

## Charts let you go a step beyond

Charts don't just tell you what to do: they also show you a picture of the end result, making it easier to understand and follow a pattern.

Knitting is an amazing activity. In bringing loops of yarn together, you create a remarkable, fluid fabric. The pieces are shaped to fit, without the waste of cutting as in woven fabrics. And the stitch patterns! From knit/purl textures to colorwork, lace, cables, and beyond, the options – ethereal or vibrant, delicate or rugged, subdued or intricate – are practically unlimited, as a stroll through any stitch dictionary will attest.

The instructions for creating knitted fabric, and in particular for the stitch patterns that elevate a project above the humdrum of stockinette or garter stitch, can be given in written or charted form. Both achieve the same end: letting you, the knitter, know how to create fabric of a particular sort. But while written instructions *tell* you what to do, charts *show* you, giving you a picture of the final result.

 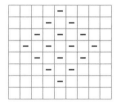

The difference between written and charted instructions couldn't be more grand. Written instructions have to be followed one word at a time. Charts replace words with symbols that resemble stitches. And while you can follow a chart symbol by symbol just as you can follow written instructions word by word, charts also let you go a step beyond: Once you see that charts arrange their symbols like the stitches of knitted fabric, **you can use charts as tools for understanding**. You can see how the parts of a stitch pattern fit together and relate to each other.

You'll soon see how understanding a stitch pattern through its chart, and comparing your knitting to the chart, can make knitting easier. You'll be better able to stay on track in your knitting, to recognize more quickly when you've gotten off track, and to get back on track with less fuss. In short, you'll be better equipped to turn loops of yarn into gorgeous knitted fabric.

## Charts are for every knitter

Novice or old hand, product knitter or process knitter, conventional knitter or idiosyncratic individual: charts are for you.

Reading charts makes sense for every knitter. No matter how long you've been knitting, learning to make sense of the symbols and how they're arranged lets you make better use of patterns given in both written and charted form. And it opens up a world of patterns given in charted form only.

What if you've tried charts before, but they've not "clicked" for you? This book will get you over that hump. It explains *why* charts are drawn as they are, taking out the mystery and leaving only clarity.

What if you're a combination knitter? Or a true lefty knitter?

*Combination knitters wrap the yarn one way for knits, and the other way for purls.*

*Lefty knitters work each row from left to right, creating new stitches on the left needle.*

Even so: charts are for you, too. Charts show which way each decrease is supposed to lean, making it easy for combination knitters to see the results they need to achieve. And lefties can follow chart rows in the direction that naturally makes sense for them.

When unconventional knitters need to read charts in a manner unlike the typical knitter, this book points out the differences. For the sake of brevity, though, the instructions in this book generally assume you knit conventionally, always forming new stitches on your right needle such that their right "legs" appear in front of the needle.

 *This book assumes you knit conventionally – but also includes tips for the unconventional knitter.*

## Charts are made simple in this book

Each of this book's six chapters clarifies one facet of reading charts.

Two chapters get you started with charts:

☀ **The Big Picture** sheds light on why charts are drawn to resemble knitted fabric, and how this governs the way you read charts.

☀ **Staying on track** suggests strategies for keeping your place within a chart, and for knitting according to a chart with a minimum of goofs.

Four chapters dive into greater detail:

☀ **Cable symbol sensibility** introduces you to the dazzling realm of cable symbols, and shows how you can unscramble them without always running to a chart's key for help.

☀ **Charts that show shape** explores the idiosyncrasies of charts shaped to match garment pieces, such as shaping implied via chart outlines only, multiple outlines for multiple sizes, and pivot stitches.

☀ **Counting stitches** dispels the notion that counting chart squares is the same as counting stitches, pointing out that paying attention to the symbols within the squares is the secret to figuring out how many stitches you ought to have on your needles.

☀ **Repeated stitches** draws parallels between the * and [] of written instructions and the repeat lines, boxes, or brackets of charted instructions, explaining how to work repeated stitch patterns flat and in the round.

Make the most out of reading this book: try the exercises suggested at the end of each chapter. **Answers to selected exercises** begin on page 92 – but don't peek until you've given the exercises a fair shot! Each is designed to strengthen your understanding of some aspect of reading charts.

Skim the **key to the symbols** commonly used in this book. It appears on page 98. Unusual symbols included just to make a specific point, however, are described on the pages where they're used.

# The Big Picture

## Charts show you The Big Picture

Everything you need to know to get started with charts stems from their resemblance to knitted fabric.

Just like written instructions, charts tell you in detail how to create knitted fabric. But a good chart does much more: it also *shows* you what that fabric is supposed to look like. It gives you The Big Picture.

Take this example. In both the photo and the chart, you see a cable crossing to the right once every 4 rows. Lace yarn overs step back and forth in two columns. Purl columns flank the lace, separating it from the cable.

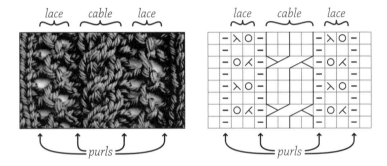

At a glance, you can see how the parts of the stitch pattern fit together. You can see, for example, that all the purl stitches are supposed to line up in columns. As you're knitting, you can watch to be sure that they do.

How does a chart show you The Big Picture? By using symbols that resemble stitches, by arranging the symbols as the stitches appear on the right side of the fabric, and by keeping clutter to a minimum.

## Symbols look like stitches

Chart symbols aren't arbitrary, random squiggles. They're meant to remind you of stitches.

When putting together charts for books, magazines, and patterns, publishers choose symbols that mimic stitches, in appearance and in width – for example:

☀ $\boxed{O}$ looks like the eyelet created by a yarn over.

☀ $\boxed{\diagdown}$ shows the right lean of a k2tog.

☀ $\boxed{\diagdown\diagup}$ is four chart squares wide because it stands for a cable cross that uses four stitches.

This helps charts look like knitted fabric. It also helps you remember what each symbol means.

The catch? Different publishers often have different ideas of what symbol best depicts a given stitch.

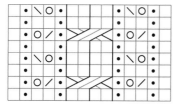
Which looks the most like a purl bump, $\boxed{-}$ or $\boxed{\bullet}$? Does $\boxed{\diagdown}$ or $\boxed{\diagup}$ best resemble a k2tog? If two symbols both remind you of a stitch, the choice becomes one of aesthetics. And different publishers make different choices.

Fortunately, getting used to a new set of symbols is often just as easy as getting used to another person's handwriting.

When starting with a new chart, **skim the chart's key**. Most likely, for each entry in the key you'll see some similarity between symbol and stitch. Take note of these similarities.

Then turn to the chart. Let the appearance of each symbol remind you of its meaning. If need be – if you encounter a symbol that leaves you in doubt – you can always refer back to the key until, gradually, all the symbols have become familiar to you.

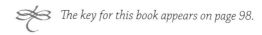 *The key for this book appears on page 98.*

## Read in the same direction you knit

Because a chart's symbols are arranged like stitches in fabric, you have to read in the same direction you knit: from the bottom up, back and forth if knitting flat or always in the same direction if knitting in the round.

Row numbers act as cues:

❊ At the chart's right edge, they mark right-side rows read from right to left.
❊ At the chart's left edge, they mark wrong-side rows read from left to right.

Row numbers that alternate between the right and left side of a chart are a hint that you should knit flat. Read back and forth, beginning at the row number and working to the other side.

*Read wrong-side rows from left to right.*

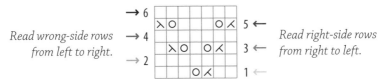

*Read right-side rows from right to left.*

Row numbers that run up the right side of the chart only are a hint that you should knit in the round. Read each row from right to left.

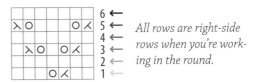

*All rows are right-side rows when you're working in the round.*

Notice that the *contents* of the above two charts are the same. Like most charts – but unlike written instructions – this same chart can be followed when knitting flat *or* when knitting in the round. Some charts hint at this dual ability by numbering just half the rows: those most easily worked on the right side.

*Rows 1, 3, and 5 are best worked as right-side rows.*

*Are you a lefty knitter? Do you create new stitches on your left needle? Then you need to read each chart row in the reverse of the usual direction: left to right for right-side rows, and right to left for wrong-side rows.*

Some charts omit alternate rows if they're very simple – for example, the wrong-side rows of many lace patterns are all purl. Keep an eye out for charts where the row numbers bump up two at a time, and look for accompanying instructions that explain what to do on the wrong-side rows.

*Pattern instructions ought to say how to work rows 2, 4, and 6.*

Remember that some stitch patterns begin with wrong-side rows! Their charts have even numbers at their right edge.

*Row 2 is a right-side row, because its row number is at the chart's right edge. So, when working flat, row 1 must be a wrong-side row.*

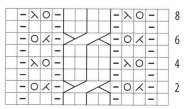

## Charts show the right side of the fabric

So that a chart can look like the right side of a piece of fabric, each symbol resembles a stitch as viewed from the right side – even if, when working flat, that stitch is worked on a wrong-side row.

Read the key to most charts, and you'll see definitions like these:

☐ Knit on RS, purl on WS

⊟ Purl on RS, knit on WS

Does this seem odd? The key is telling you to work ☐ and ⊟ differently on right- and wrong-side rows. But it makes perfect sense when you consider this: every symbol shows you a stitch **as viewed from the right side of the fabric**.

Viewing each stitch from the right side lets a chart look like fabric. It lets you see the strong vertical lines of k2, p2 rib, and the pebbly surface of seed stitch.

**K2, p2 rib**

**Seed stitch**

☐ Knit on RS, purl on WS

⊟ Purl on RS, knit on WS

You might be tempted to ask, "But wouldn't it be easier if I always knit when I saw ☐, and always purled when I saw ⊟?" Ah, but here's the catch:

**K2, p2 rib**

**Seed stitch**

☐ Knit

⊟ Purl

When ☐ means "knit" and ⊟ means "purl" on all rows, the rib chart *no longer looks like ribbing*: the vertical nature of the stitch pattern has disappeared. The seed stitch chart *no longer looks like seed stitch*: the pebbly surface has been replaced by thin vertical lines. You've lost The Big Picture. And you can't follow these charts in the round – they're only good for knitting flat.

So that charts can show the right side of the fabric, every symbol has **one meaning**: the appearance of a stitch on the right side of the fabric. But you may need **two means** to achieve that appearance: one when working on the right side, and another when working on the wrong side.

Consider ☐ and ⊟. They're the symbols you'll see most frequently on wrong-side rows.

☐ Knit on RS, purl on WS     To get the smooth, plain, ☐ appearance of a knit stitch on the right side of the fabric, you have to purl when working a wrong-side row.

⊟ Purl on RS, knit on WS     To get a ⊟ purl bump to appear on on the right side, you have to knit on the wrong side.

The key on page 98 shows that a few other symbols are also worked differently on right- and wrong-side rows.

Usually, this isn't a big deal. You don't have to figure out the wrong-side approach for lots of symbols, since most stitch patterns only have knits and purls on wrong-side rows. Increases, decreases, cable crosses, and other maneuvers are often done on right-side rows only.

 *The trick is to remember that each symbol shows what you ought to see on the right side. When working wrong-side rows, ask yourself: what do I need to do, to match what the symbols show on the right side?*

## Blank squares keep clutter to a minimum

Symbols that show the right-side view of a stitch are just one part of getting charts to look like fabric. Another is keeping clutter to a minimum. And for that, many charts use blank ☐ squares for the "background" stitch pattern.

When every square of a chart is filled with a symbol, the result can look "busy" or cluttered. It can be hard to discern the patterning.

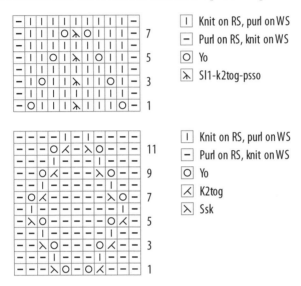

What's going on with these charts? What should the fabric look like?

To make the patterning more apparent, many charts use blank ☐ squares for the predominant stitch pattern, called the "background" stitch pattern. Often, it's stockinette: knit on the right side, purl on the wrong side.

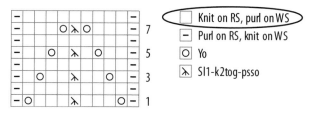

Here, the horseshoe lace pattern shows up clearly when blank squares stand for stockinette.

But you can't assume ☐ stands for stockinette. Sometimes, the background stitch pattern is reverse stockinette: purl on the right side, knit on the wrong side.

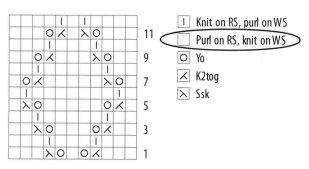

These lacy vines "pop" when blank squares stand for reverse stockinette.

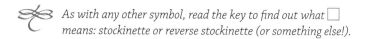 As with any other symbol, read the key to find out what ☐ means: stockinette or reverse stockinette (or something else!).

## Special charts come with special instructions

Some kinds of knitting aren't served well by typical charts. Instead, to portray the fabric compactly and clearly, their charts are often drawn in their own quirky way. Rest assured that accompanying instructions explain how to follow these off-kilter charts.

Mosaic knitting is a classic example. Each row of a mosaic chart matches *two* rows of knitting.

 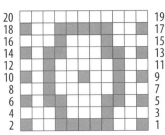

Cast on with light yarn and knit one row. Work each row of the chart twice, alternating two rows using dark yarn with two rows using light yarn.

On light rows:

☐ Knit

▣ Slip with yarn held to WS

On dark rows:

☐ Slip with yarn held to WS

▣ Knit

Double knitting is another good example. Each square in a two-color double-knitting chart matches *two* stitches, one on each "face" of the double-sided fabric.

 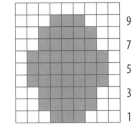

Work each square of the chart twice, as follows:

☐ On RS, k1 light and p1 dark; on WS, k1 dark and p1 light

▣ On RS, k1 dark and p1 light; on WS, k1 light and p1 dark

Hold unused color to back when knitting, to front when purling.

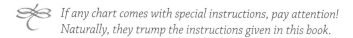 *If any chart comes with special instructions, pay attention! Naturally, they trump the instructions given in this book.*

If these charts were drawn in the typical fashion, with one chart row per row of knitting and one symbol per stitch, they would take up more space. More to the point: they wouldn't look much like the fabric. The mosaic chart would be cluttered with symbols for purl and slip stitches. The double-knitting chart would show vertical stripes instead of a circle.

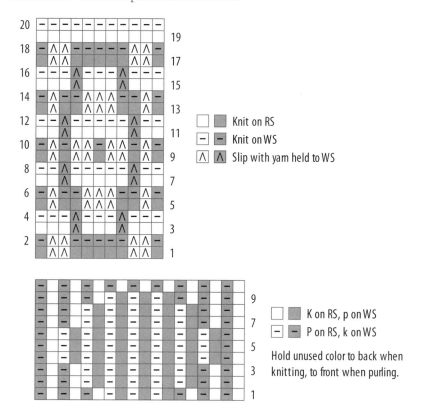

☐ ▨ Knit on RS

⊟ ▨ Knit on WS

⟨∧⟩ ▨ Slip with yarn held to WS

☐ ▨ K on RS, p on WS

⊟ ▨ P on RS, k on WS

Hold unused color to back when knitting, to front when purling.

## Tweak your charts to your liking

As you've probably guessed by now, any chart can be drawn in more than one way. So if you don't like the way a chart looks – if its symbols don't remind you of stitches, or you simply find it irksome to read – then fix it. Colorize it, redraw it, or enlarge it.

Suppose you find a chart a little too cluttered and jumbled to read.

| ☐ | K on RS, p on WS |
| ☐ | P on RS, k on WS |

Use a highlighter pen to colorize some symbols and make them "pop."

| ☐ | K on RS, p on WS |
| ◢ | P on RS, k on WS |

Or redraw it with alternate symbols. Try blank ☐ squares for the background stitch pattern – in this case, stockinette. Pencil, eraser, and dime-store graph paper are all you need.

| ☐ | K on RS, p on WS |
| ☐ | P on RS, k on WS |

Colorizing is a great option for colorwork charts presented in black and white, with arbitrary symbols like +, #, and ◇ standing in for colors.

+ olive
# rust
◇ mustard

With highlighters that mimic the yarn colors you plan to use, bring the colorwork pattern into view.

+ olive
# rust
◇ mustard

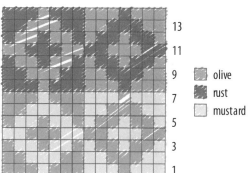

Or make the pattern clearer yet by redrawing it with colored pencils.

olive
rust
mustard

Another way to tweak your charts is to enlarge those that are too small to read. See page 60 for more tips along these lines.

Colorizing, redrawing, or enlarging a chart might take a few minutes – but it's time well spent, if it makes your knitting time more pleasant.

# Summary

❋ A good chart shows you The Big Picture, the fabric that following the chart will create. This lets you see how the parts of the stitch pattern fit together, making it easier to learn and follow the pattern. It also means you read charts in the same direction you knit: from the bottom up, back and forth if knitting flat or always in the same direction if knitting in the round.

❋ Remember that a chart shows the right side of the fabric, so on wrong-side rows you have to work the stitches with an eye towards creating the correct appearance on the right side.

❋ Don't let a chart throw you: review its key, read any instructions that come with it, and – if other symbols would make more sense to you – redraw it.

Test your understanding of The Big Picture with these exercises:

1. Match each of these charts to its swatch photo.

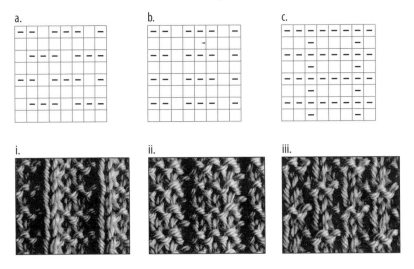

a.   b.   c.

i.   ii.   iii.

2. Cast on 8 stitches, and try knitting from the above charts. Does your knitting resemble the charts?

3. Open up a few knitting books and magazines, and see what symbols they use for common stitches like knit, purl, yarn over, k2tog, and slip. How are they similar? How do they differ? Which remind you of stitches? Which do you prefer, and why?

# Staying on track

## Notice how the design elements line up

The first step in using a chart to stay on track is looking the chart over. Notice how the parts of the stitch pattern – its yarn overs, decreases, purls, bobbles, and so on – line up in relation to each other. Do they stack in columns, or layer in rows? Do they fit together like the blocks of a checkerboard, or the bricks in a wall? Or do they connect in some other way?

Consider these sample charts:

Here, a diamond of seed stitch sits within a square of stockinette. The diamond begins with a single purl stitch, and grows two stitches wider on each row until it's seven stitches wide. Then it narrows by two stitches on each row until it's a single purl stitch again.

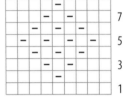

For this cable, crosses occur on every other right-side row. The crosses alternate direction: a left cross is followed four rows later by a right cross, then vice versa as rows 1-8 are repeated.

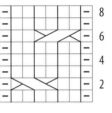

Decreases stack in a column at the right edge of this chart. The matching yarn overs, however, run along a diagonal: each is one stitch to the right of the yarn over worked two rows previously.

Becoming familiar with a stitch pattern in this way often lets you avoid the tedium of reading a chart stitch by stitch. It works especially well for knit/purl patterns, for cables, and for simple lace patterns. Sometimes, you can even memorize a stitch pattern and leave its chart behind.

But don't take the charts for more elaborate lace patterns too literally. It can be difficult for a chart based on a grid of straight lines to portray a sinuous lace pattern with strict fidelity. For example, yarn overs that line up vertically in a chart may actually line up diagonally in the knitted fabric.

## Cover the rows you have not yet knit

Placing a straightedge on your chart lets your eye follow smoothly along a row. Be sure to place it *above* your current row, so you can compare the current row to the previous rows.

---

Feel free to use whatever you find convenient as a straightedge. Try these options, or come up with your own solutions:

* Lay a ruler or scrap of paper on top of your chart.

* Fasten an index card to your chart with a paper clip.

* Place a sticky note on your chart. Or try a bit of highlighter tape: brightly colored, translucent tape that sticks, peels up, and sticks again several times before losing its stickiness. Both are available at office supply stores.

* Hold your chart to a metal board with a magnetic strip. Your local yarn shop might stock "mag boards" for this purpose. Or you can improvise with a cookie sheet – a handy option for large charts, as described on page 61.

Be sure to **cover the rows you have not yet knit,** leaving your current row and the previous rows exposed. This lets you see how the stitches of the current row line up compared with those of the previous rows.

Suppose, for example, you're working row 3 of the diamond chart on the previous page.

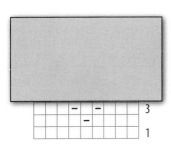

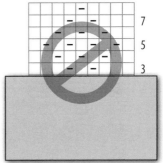

*Covering rows 4-8 leaves rows 1-3 visible. As you're working row 3, you can see that its two purl stitches are supposed to line up on each side of the purl stitch created on row 2.*

*Whoops! Covering rows 1 and 2 means you can't see how the stitches of row 3 are supposed to line up with the stitches of row 2.*

## Keep track of each chart separately

Following multiple charts is a little like patting your head with one hand while rubbing your belly with the other – only easier, because you can focus on each chart in turn.

It's not uncommon for a pattern to contain more than one chart, and instructions like these:

Cast on 98 sts. Work in k1, p1 rib for 1½" (4 cm). Next WS row, establish pattern as follows: work 34 sts Moss st, 6 sts Left Cross Rope, 18 sts Staghorn Cable, 6 sts Right Cross Rope, 34 sts Moss st.

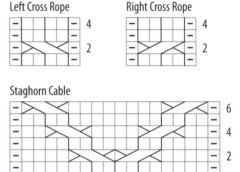

Do yourself a favor: *before* knitting from the charts, count stitches and place clip-on markers or bits of waste yarn between the various sections – that way, you don't have to knit and count at the same time. You can even label each section with a paper hang tag, so you know where to follow each chart.

Remember to work the charts in the correct order on each row. If you work Left Cross Rope *first* on wrong-side rows, you'll need to work it *last* on right-side rows.

*Work the charts in this order on wrong-side rows.* ⟶

Left Cross Rope    Staghorn Cable    Right Cross Rope

⟵ *Work in the opposite order on right-side rows.*

Unless all the charts are the same height, you'll reach a point where you're working different rows. For example, after completing row 4 of the charts shown here, you'll continue with row 5 of the taller chart but move to row 1 of the shorter charts. You'll then move on to rows 6 and 2, and so on. Be sure to keep tabs on your current row for *each* chart. Use sticky notes, bits of highlighter tape, or magnetic strips, as described on page 25 – whatever works for you.

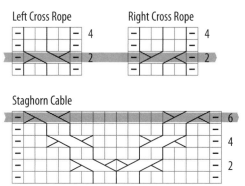

You may even need to keep track of different sections within the same chart. Consider this example:

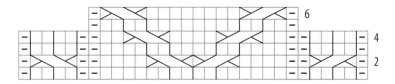

Three charts have been melded into one, making it easier to see their combined effect and to remember in which order to work them on right- and wrong-side rows. Yet the combined chart's sections are different heights. As if the sections were separate, keep track of your current row within each section separately.

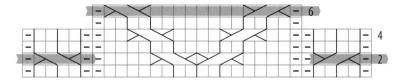

## Compare your knitting to the chart

Frequently checking your knitting against the chart assures you all is well, or – if you have goofed – lets you notice the goof soon after it's made, while it's still easy to fix.

Suppose you're knitting a seed-stitch diamond within a larger expanse of stockinette. Stitch markers point out which stitches are being worked according to the chart. Are you on track?

While looking at the right side of the fabric, compare the stitches you've just created to the symbols of your **current** chart row.

 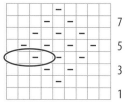

*The newest stitches – those on the needle attached to the yarn – seem to match up okay with the first few symbols of row 5: three knits alternating with two purls.*

Compare the stitches you have yet to work to the symbols of the **previous** chart row.

 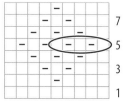

*But the stitches on the other needle seem a little off-kilter: two purls and two knits ought to be a knit, a purl, and two knits.*

Stop knitting right away if you notice a mismatch – don't keep going, hoping that things will work out. Figure out what happened, and backtrack if need be.

Of course, the advice to check your knitting against its chart only makes sense if you can "read" your knitting. The next page explains how.

## Teach yourself to read your knitting

Are you unsure of how to read your knitting? Do you have a tough time distinguishing between, say, a knit stitch and a k2tog? The process of learning to read your knitting is simple: Knit. Look. Repeat.

Let's say you want to learn to spot an ssk in your knitting. Work an ssk, then stop and look at it. *While you know what you have just done*, figure out what makes that ssk look different from other stitches. Pick out the visual cues that say to you, "Okay, that's an ssk. Not a knit stitch or a k2tog, but an ssk."

stitch created by working ssk

two stitches worked together, with the right stitch leaning to the left and sitting on top of the left stitch

Now knit a few more stitches, and look at your knitting again. Can you still spot the ssk?

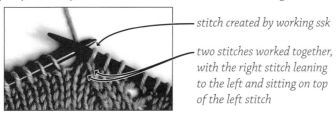

There it is!

Work a couple more rows. Find that ssk again. What visual cues tell you it's been two rows since you worked that ssk?

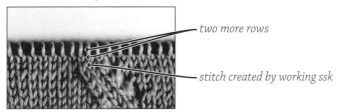

two more rows

stitch created by working ssk

*Keep looking at your knitting* when you know what you've just done. Practice recognizing various kinds of stitches. Soon enough, you'll be able to read your knitting with ease.

## Get back on track

Suppose you've lost your place in your knitting. Use your charts to get back on track: compare the stitches that you worked most recently to the symbols in the charts.

Start by identifying the stitches that you worked last. They're the ones attached to the working yarn. Also, figure out if they were worked as part of a right- or wrong-side row: with the right side of the fabric facing you, consider where the yarn ended up, and in what direction that row must have been knit.

*Still attached to the yarn, these circled stitches were worked most recently. They were worked from right to left, as part of a right-side row. Voilà! You've just eliminated half the chart rows – the wrong-side rows – from consideration.*

With the right side still facing you, take a closer look at the stitches. How were they worked?

*Most recently, ☐ O ☐ ⟨ was worked.*

*Lefty knitters, remember your rows run in opposite the usual direction: from left to right for right-side rows, and from right to left for wrong-side rows.*

Now turn to your chart. Where in the chart do the symbols for those stitches appear?

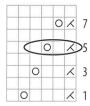 *O ⋏ appears at the beginning of row 5, a right-side row. So, you're in the middle of row 5, and you need to k2 to complete row 5.*

What if your just-knit stitches appear more than once in the chart? Consider the surrounding stitches, and how they compare to the chart.

*The stitches worked most recently were part of a wrong-side row. How do you know? The yarn is attached to the left needle.*

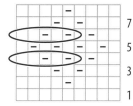 *The ⎯ ⎯ stitches on the needles match wrong-side rows 4 and 6 of the chart. But the stitches of the previous row match row 5, not row 3. So, you're in the middle of row 6.*

# Summary

❊ Go beyond reading a chart stitch by stitch: notice how its design elements line up in relation to each other. That way, you'll need to refer to the chart less often.

❊ Cover the rows you have not yet knit, so you can see how your current row relates to the previous rows.

❊ While you know what stitches you have just created, look at your knitting frequently and learn to recognize the individual stitches.

❊ When you do get lost, match the stitches on your needles to the symbols of the chart. This will help you find your place and get back on track.

Use these exercises to practice techniques for staying on track:

1. Of the following statements, which are accurate descriptions of the chart shown here? Which are false?

    a. A panel of stockinette-based lace, 6 stitches wide, is flanked by columns of purl stitches.

    b. Lace patterning takes place on every right-side row.

    c. In the lower half of the chart, a line of three yarn overs runs diagonally from the lower right to the upper left. Matching k2tog form a line to the left of the yarn overs.

    d. In the upper half of the chart, yarn overs and k2tog run diagonally from the lower left to the upper right.

| | | | | | | | | |
|---|---|---|---|---|---|---|---|---|
| − | | | O | | | ⊼ | − | 15 |
| − | | | | | | | − | |
| − | | O | | | ⊼ | | − | 13 |
| − | | | | | | | − | |
| − | O | | | ⊼ | | | − | 11 |
| − | | | | | | | − | |
| − | | | | | | | − | 9 |
| − | | | | | | | − | |
| − | ⋋ | | | O | | | − | 7 |
| − | | | | | | | − | |
| − | | ⋋ | | | O | | − | 5 |
| − | | | | | | | − | |
| − | | | ⋋ | | | O | − | 3 |
| − | | | | | | | − | |
| − | | | | | | | − | 1 |

2. This sample is being knit according the chart shown above. Which row is currently being knit? How can you tell?

# Cable symbol sensibility

## Cable patterns are made up of crossed stitches

Working stitches out of their usual order – traditionally with the help of a cable needle – crosses them, with some stitches lying over other stitches. These cable crosses combine to create stitch patterns with lots of textural appeal.

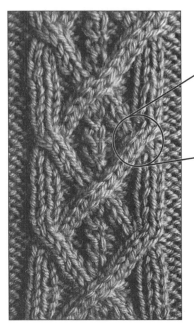

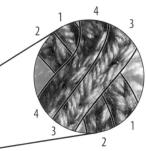

In this cable cross, stitches that would normally be worked in order from 1 through 4 are instead crossed and worked out of order: 3 and 4 before 1 and 2.

 *Charts are an excellent way to depict cable patterns, as they show how the crossed stitches of each row flow into the crosses of neighboring rows.*

## Stitches can be crossed in many ways

Crossing a few stitches or many stitches, to the left or to the right, makes possible dozens of basic cable crosses. Unique crosses result from working some stitches not as knits, but as purls or in some other manner.

Most of the crosses in a typical cable pattern are composed of two groups of stitches, called "strands."

Some crosses have three strands: the outer strands exchange places while the center strand remains in the middle.

If the top strand of a cross moves up and to the left, it's called a left cross.

If the top strand moves up and to the right, it's a right cross.

Each strand may contain just one stitch – like the strands in this example – or multiple stitches.

The stitches can be knit, purled, or worked in some other manner for special effect. Here, a knitted strand crosses over a purled strand.

## Cable symbols come in a variety of flavors

Open a half-dozen knitting books, and you're likely to find nearly a half-dozen ways to draw cable symbols. Some do a better job of resembling knitted fabric, which can make it easier to grasp the gist of a chart at a glance. Others more clearly represent unusual cable crosses, such as those incorporating increases, decreases, or twisted stitches. Yet each cable symbol in some way looks like a cable cross, showing its width and crossing direction.

Outlines can trace cable strands, setting them apart from the background fabric and from each other.

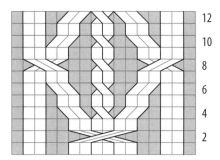

Purls can be shown by shading.

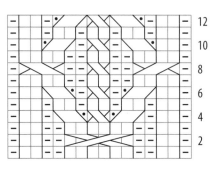

Or purls can be shown by dots or dashes. Either way, slanted outlines show the direction of a cross.

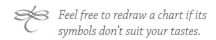

*Feel free to redraw a chart if its symbols don't suit your tastes.*

In "lightning bolt" symbols, a short diagonal line shows the direction of the cross.

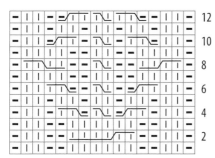

The top horizontal line shows the width of the top strand, and the bottom line shows the width of the rest of the cross. Symbols within the chart squares show how to work each stitch.

Yet another approach represents each knit stitch of a cross directly, with its own diagonal line. Other slanted figures indicate if stitches are to be purled, knit through the back loop to twist, or worked in some other special way.

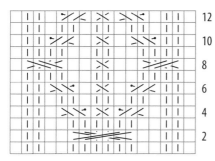

To match the cable symbols, plain vertical lines stand for uncrossed knit stitches. To keep clutter to a minimum, blank squares stand for purls.

## You don't have to be tied to a chart's key

Because cable symbols look like cable crosses, you don't need to refer to a chart's key each time you run across a cable symbol. Instead, you can usually figure out what a cable symbol means just by looking at it.

Start by skimming over the key. Check out the way it shows purl stitches. Stay on the lookout for unusual cable crosses. The point is not to memorize every symbol, but just to get to know them a bit better, so you can make sense of them with confidence.

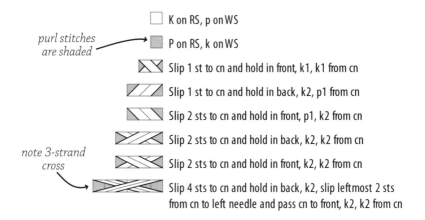

Then turn to the chart. Note the width of each strand. If a strand travels, see if it travels over a background of stockinette, reverse stockinette, or some other stitch pattern. Noticing details like these lets you tease meaning from a cable symbol. And when a symbol is seated within the context of a chart, this meaning is easier to discern than when the symbol is standing solo in a key.

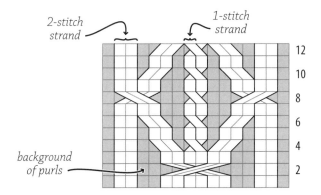

Now you're ready to decipher the chart's cable symbols. For each, ask:

☀ How many strands does the cross have?

☀ How many stitches are in each strand?

☀ How do the strands cross?

☀ How are the stitches worked?

The answers tell you precisely how to work the cable cross.

## How many strands does the cross have?

A two-strand cross swaps one group of stitches over another. A three-strand cross swaps two outer strands over a third strand that stays put in the middle. Most cable symbols clearly show how many strands are in the cross.

Seeing whether a cable cross has two or three strands is straightforward if its symbol outlines the strands, or indicates stitches with diagonal lines.

Count outlined strands, including the background strand.

2 strands     2 strands     3 strands

Count groups of parallel diagonal lines.

2 strands     2 strands     3 strands

For lightning-bolt symbols, distinguishing between two- and three-strand crosses is a little trickier. Usually you can tell from context.

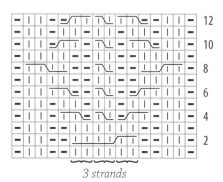

3 strands

Does  stand for a two-strand cross (two stitches crossed over four), or a three-strand cross (three strands of two stitches each)? Look at the chart: the six stitches at the center of row 2 split apart into three strands on row 4, so the cross on row 2 is most likely a three-strand cross.

*When in doubt, refer to the chart's key.*

## How many stitches are in each strand?

Look to the width of each strand shown within a cable symbol, or – better yet – look to the symbol's surroundings within a chart. Then count chart squares.

With some cable symbols, counting the stitches in each strand is a snap.

Other symbols are easier to read when shown within a chart.

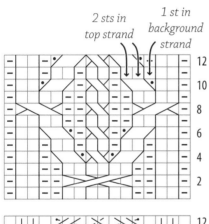

*2 sts in top strand* · *1 st in background strand*

How wide are the strands in 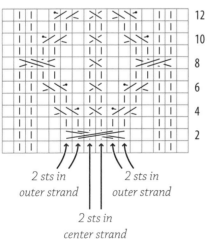? Placed in a chart, it's clear that a top strand of two stitches crosses over a background strand of a single stitch.

On its own, ⟨symbol⟩ seems a little jumbled. In a chart, each strand reveals itself as two stitches wide.

*2 sts in outer strand* · *2 sts in center strand* · *2 sts in outer strand*

## How do the strands cross?

Crossing stitches with the help of a cable needle means transferring some stitches to the cable needle and temporarily holding them out of the way while working other stitches. Cable symbols help you visualize which stitches to place on hold, and where to hold them.

Imagine pulling cable strands like you were pulling taffy. You can pull strands off the left needle, cross them, and work them in their new order onto the right needle.

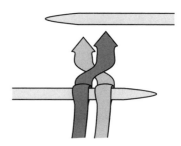

Now picture these same crossed strands layered on top of a cable symbol.

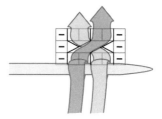

The symbol shows, in a very small space, how the strands cross.

## Two-strand crosses have three steps

No matter the number of stitches in each strand or how they're worked, the same three steps will get you a two-strand cross.

To work a two-strand cross:

1. place a strand on hold to front or back,
2. work the stitches of the other strand, then
3. work the stitches of the strand on hold.

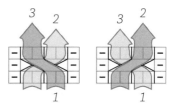

The question is, do you hold the cable needle in front or in back? How can you tell?

Look to the stitches at the bottom right of the cable symbol. They form the strand that gets placed on the cable needle. Now look to the symbol's outlines, lightning bolt, or diagonal lines. They show whether that strand crosses over or under – and that tells you where to hold the cable needle.

These symbols show you need to hold the first strand to the **front**, so it can cross **over** the other strand.

These symbols show you need to hold the first strand to the **back**, so it can cross **under** the other strand.

 *Lefty knitters, look to the bottom **left** of the cable symbol. That portion of the symbol matches the strand you'll place on your cable needle, as you work a right-side row from left to right.*

## Three-strand crosses have five steps

Three-strand crosses are much the same as two-strand crosses, except for extra steps that handle the center strand. These extra steps can sandwich the center strand between the other two strands, or hide it underneath them both. Placing it at the very bottom of the pile – as described below – lets you create reversible fabric out of cabled ribbing.

To work a three-strand cross:

1. place the first outer strand on hold,
2. place the center strand on hold to the back,
3. work the stitches of the second outer strand,
4. work the stitches of the center strand, then
5. work the stitches of the first outer strand.

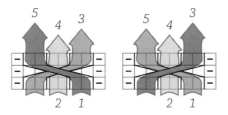

Again, look to the cable symbol to see whether to hold the first outer strand to front or back.

 *Lefty knitters, remember that the outer strand you'll encounter first will be on the left side of the cable symbol. Look to the bottom left of the symbol to figure out if that strand should be held to the front or back.*

These symbols show that you need to hold the first outer strand to the **front**, so it can cross **over** the other strands. Hold the center strand to the back on a second cable needle. Then work the second outer strand from the left needle, the center strand from the back cable needle, and the first outer strand from the front cable needle.

These symbols show that you need to hold the first outer strand to the **back**, so it can cross **under** the other outer strand. Hold the center strand to the back on the same cable needle, and work the second outer strand from the left needle. Then slip the center strand to the left needle and move the cable needle to the **front** so the first outer strand crosses **over** the center strand. Work the center strand from the left needle, then the first outer strand from the cable needle.

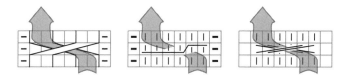

## How are the stitches worked?

You could spend years exploring cable patterns with plain vanilla crosses: just knits crossed over knits, or knits crossed over purls. More flavorful cables, though, sometimes cross increases, decreases, twisted stitches, or other stitches.

Take this faggoted cable, for example.

On right-side rows without a cable cross, the four stitches at the heart of the cable are k2, yo, ssk. This pattern continues on the crossing rows: stitches are crossed, then worked as k2, yo, ssk.

Just as cable symbols have different ways of representing purl stitches – such as shaded squares, dots, or dashes – they also have different ways of telling you when to abandon bland knits and purls in favor of something a little spicier. Three examples below reveal three options for charting this faggoted cable.

If a chart outlines each cable strand, it may squeeze embellishments within the outlines to convey how you should work the stitches. Read these embellishments from right to left – that is, in the direction you're knitting.

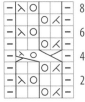

Here, the embellishments within the ⊠○◁ symbol on row 4 mimic the ⊠○☐ symbols on rows 2, 6, and 8. After placing two stitches on hold in front, you would knit two stitches from the left needle, then yo, ssk from the cable needle.

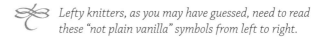
Lightning-bolt symbols shine with refreshing clarity by placing mini-symbols within the chart squares.

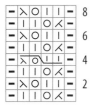 Just read from right to left, working the stitches of a cross according to these mini-symbols.

When diagonal lines represent crossed knit stitches, exaggerated, elongated, and slanted symbols represent other sorts of crossed stitches. Read these slanted symbols from right to left *along the top* of a cable symbol.

 For example, the stylized ssk symbol within ⊐✳⫣ spans four chart squares, with its two "legs" at the bottom of the squares on the right. But it extends to the very top left of the cable symbol, indicating that working an ssk is the last part of completing the cable cross.

| uncrossed, reading right to left: | | crossed, reading right to left along top of symbol: | |
|---|---|---|---|
| ⋋O⏽⏽ | *k2* | ⊐✳⫣ | *k2 from left needle* |
| ⋋O⏽⏽ | *yo* | ⊐✳⫣ | *yo* |
| ⋋O⏽⏽ | *ssk* | ⊐✳⫣ | *ssk from cn* |

## Summary

❋ Despite the huge number of possible cable crosses, and many possible ways of drawing cable symbols, each set of cable symbols makes sense in its own way.

❋ Because the symbols look like cable crosses – showing the cable strands and how they cross – you can learn to decipher the cable symbols within a chart after just skimming over its key.

❋ You can still peek at the key if an unusual symbol puzzles you – but you don't have to go running to the key for *every* symbol.

Test your ability to decipher cable symbols with these exercises:

1. For these crosses, is the cable needle held in front or in back?

    a. 

    b. 

    c. 

2. Match each of these symbols to its definition.

    a. 

    b. 

    c. 

    d. 

    e. 

    f. 

    i.   Slip 3 sts to cn and hold in back, k1, k3 from cn

    ii.  Slip 3 sts to cn and hold in back, k2, slip leftmost st from cn to left needle and pass cn to front, p1, k2 from cn

    iii. Slip 1 st to cn and hold in back, k3, k1 from cn

    iv.  Slip 3 sts to cn and hold in front, k1, k3 from cn

    v.   Slip 2 sts to cn and hold in front, slip 1 st to second cn and hold in back, k2, p1 from back cn, k2 from front cn

    vi.  Slip 1 st to cn and hold in front, k3, k1 from cn

# Charts that show shape

# Not all charts are rectangular

Some charts mimic the shape of a knitted piece, such as a mitten hand, a pullover front, or a wedge of a tam or triangular shawl.

At a glance, you can tell this is a chart for a pullover front. You can see its shirt-tail hem, its armholes geared for set-in sleeves, its opening for a polo collar, and its shoulder shaping. The chart differs from a schematic in that it doesn't show dimensions. Rather, it shows every stitch.

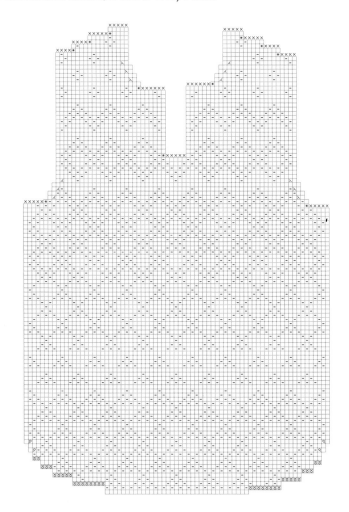

# Patterning fills the space

Showing every stitch in a knitted piece has a big bonus: it lets a chart show you exactly how the piece is patterned. You get to see how color or texture fills its every nook and cranny.

Symmetrical swirls and a checkered band fill this mitten chart, even as the top of the chart narrows to match the shape of the mitten hand.

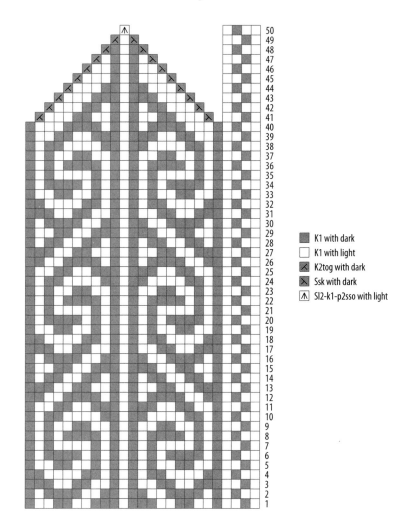

■ K1 with dark
□ K1 with light
◪ K2tog with dark
◪ Ssk with dark
▲ Sl2-k1-p2sso with light

## Symbols explain precisely how to shape fabric

Using symbols like $⟋$, $○$, and $×$, a chart gives stitch-by-stitch instructions for knitting a garment piece to a specific shape.

Knitters have many ways of shaping fabric:

☀ Decreases and bind-offs narrow the fabric.

☀ Increases and cast-ons widen the fabric.

☀ Short rows add length in a selected portion of the fabric.

Chart symbols show exactly how to shape fabric in these ways – for example, which decreases to use, and where to place them. At the same time, the outline of a chart shows the resulting shape.

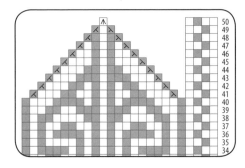

Paired decreases narrow the tip of this mitten hand.

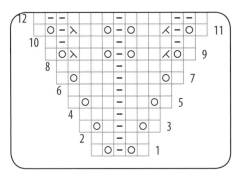

Increases widen this wedge of a triangular shawl.

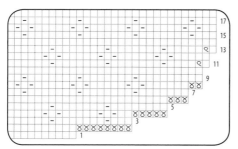

Cast-on stitches shape this shirttail. Note they appear at the ends of rows – for example, you'll work to the end of row 2, cast 8 stitches onto your right needle, then turn and work those 8 stitches at the beginning of row 3.

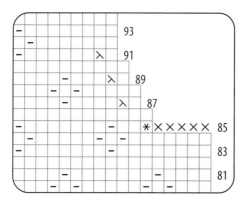

Bind-offs shape this underarm. Remember that binding off 5 stitches actually "uses up" 6 stitches. So after binding off at the beginning of row 85, you'll have one stitch on your right needle, as indicated by the ✱ symbol. Then you'll need to k2 (*not* k3!) before your first purl.

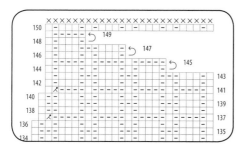

Short rows shape this shoulder, resulting in a smooth bind-off edge. At each "wrap and turn" symbol, you'll wrap a stitch, turn while unworked stitches remain on your left needle, and work back in the other direction.

 *Lefty knitters, you'll need to tweak charts that show cast-ons, bind-offs, or short-row turns. Move those symbols up or down a row, so cast-ons and turns occur at the **ends** of rows (in the direction **you** work them), and bind-offs occur at the **beginnings** of rows.*

## Sometimes shaping symbols are omitted

To reduce clutter, some charts show shaping not with symbols, but just with their outlines. Accompanying written instructions may give details – for example, which increases or decreases to use – or the choice may be left up to you.

By itself, the outline of this chart shows that you need to decrease on rounds 41 through 50. But it doesn't specify what decreases to use. The mitten's pattern might say where to use k2tog decreases and where to use ssk decreases. Or the pattern might leave the decreases as "knitter's choice."

## Multiple outlines match multiple sizes

Shaping symbols are often omitted when a single chart represents multiple sizes, each confined within its own outline.

This excerpt of a chart for a sleeve has outlines for three sizes. The sleeve is pretty much the same for all the sizes, just a bit wider for sizes M and L.

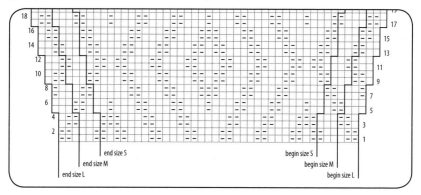

To follow a chart like this, ignore anything that falls outside the outline for your size. For example, when knitting a size S sleeve, you would pay attention to just this portion of the chart.

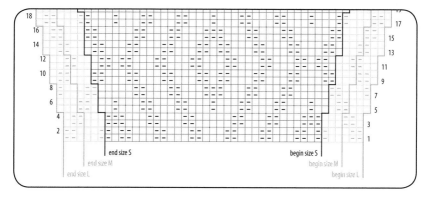

 *Remember to follow any special instructions that accompany the chart. They may tell you how to shape the fabric, or how to handle selvedge stitches.*

## Pirouette on the pivot stitches

A chart for a wide, symmetrical piece sometimes shows just *half* of the piece, as if it had been folded. At the fold, the chart marks either the center of the piece (if the stitch count is even) or a central "pivot" stitch (if the stitch count is odd). For each row of knitting, you'll work across the corresponding row of the chart *twice*: once for each folded layer.

---

Compare this chart to those on page 55. Rather than show the right half of the sleeve and the mirror-image left half, it shows just the right half. And it shows the sleeve's center stitch, marked on the chart as a "pivot st."

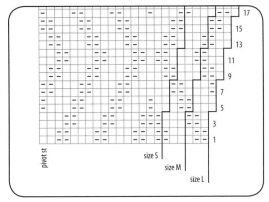

To follow this chart, read each row from its outside edge to the pivot stitch and back out again. That is, for row 1, for size L:

❈ Work from the right edge to the pivot stitch: p2, k3, p2, k1, [p2, k3] twice, p2, k1.

❈ Work the pivot stitch *just once*: k1.

❈ And work back to the right edge: k1, [p2, k3] twice, p2, k1, p2, k3, p2.

Row 2 is the same *except* it's a wrong-side row, so ☐ means purl and ⊟ means knit:

❈ Work from the right edge to the pivot stitch: k2, p3, k2, p1, [k2, p3] twice, k2, p1.

❈ Work the pivot stitch *just once*: p1.

❈ And work back to the right edge: p1, [k2, p3] twice, k2, p1, k2, p3, k2.

Reading each row of the chart twice is just one aspect of pirouetting on the pivot stitches. To truly unfold such a chart, you may also have to mirror-image some stitches.

Increases and decreases often come in mirror-image pairs. Here are some examples.

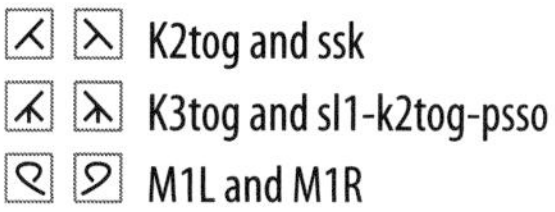
K2tog and ssk
K3tog and sl1-k2tog-psso
M1L and M1R

This excerpt shows a portion of a lace chart, perhaps for a triangular lace shawl. Here's how you would read row 9:

- Work from the right edge to the pivot stitch: k1, yo, *k2tog,* k2, yo.
- Work the pivot stitch: p1.
- And work back to the right edge, mirror-imaging the stitches: yo, k2, *ssk,* yo, k1.

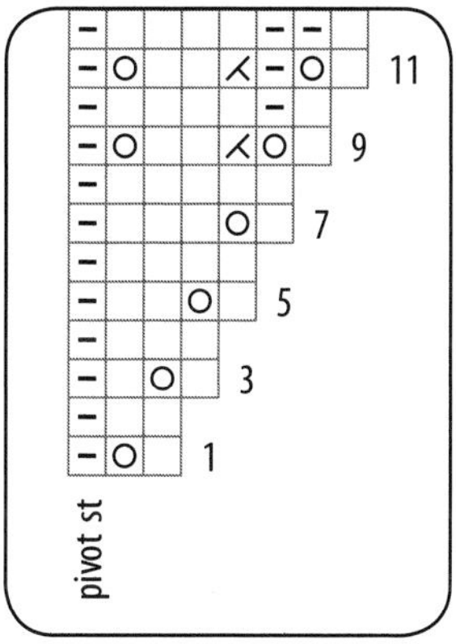
11
9
7
5
3
1
pivot st

Of course, **you can always redraw a chart**, showing both its mirror-image halves, if that would make it easier for you to follow the chart.

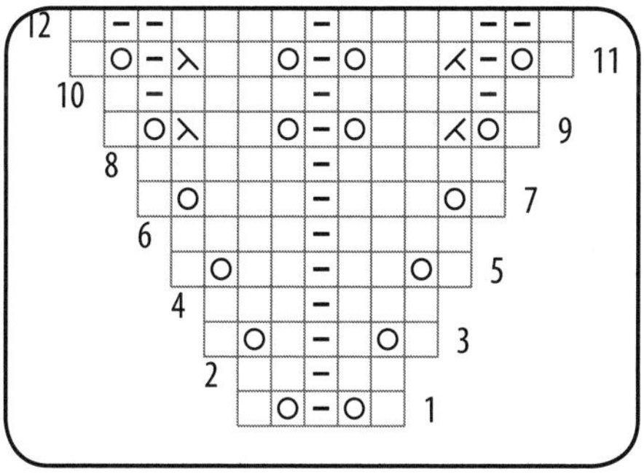
12
11
10
9
8
7
6
5
4
3
2
1

# Mind the gap!

Does a gap in a chart mean you'll have a gap in your knitting? Common sense will give you the answer.

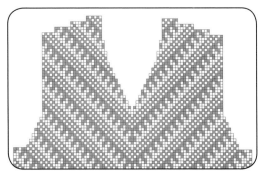

The gap in this chart shows a V-neck opening in a pullover front. Work the left front and right front separately, each with its own supply of yarn.

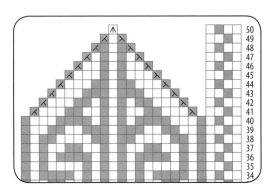

But the gap in this mitten chart does *not* show a gap in your knitting. Instead, the gap merely shows where stitches have been decreased away. Work continuously across each row of the chart, ignoring the gap in the chart.

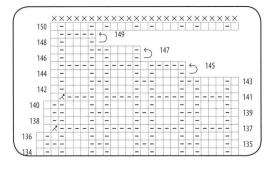

Likewise, the gap in this chart does *not* show a gap in your knitting. Stitches left unworked at the end of short rows 144, 146, and 148 are later worked on row 150.

Why would a chart contain a gap, even if the knitting doesn't? So that, within each section of the chart, the patterning can flow smoothly from stitch to stitch, matching the knitting.

Clearly, in rounds 40 and below of this chart, the border that runs alongside this mitten hand features a mini-checkerboard stripe, just two stitches wide.

But in rounds 41 and above, the border is distorted. The checkerboard stripe is obscured because the stitches of the border aren't stacked on top of each other. Without a gap next to the line of decreases, the chart doesn't resemble the knitted fabric.

Compare this chart to the one in the center of the previous page. Can you see how the gap in that chart preserves the patterning of the border?

## Safeguard your sanity

A chart that shows an entire garment piece is likely to be many rows wide and many rows tall. When printed in a limited space, those squares are likely to be tiny. Don't go blind or crazy trying to decipher tiny little squares – safeguard your sanity with these tips.

You can always photocopy and enlarge a chart to make it more legible.

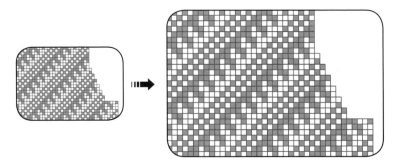

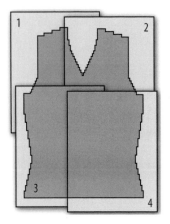

If a photocopy spans multiple pieces of paper, tape them together. This lets you follow continuously across each row of the chart.

With very large charts, a straightedge is especially helpful for reading across your current row without accidently wandering into neighboring rows. Your local yarn shop might have magnetic boards designed for this purpose. If not – or if your chart is bigger than any commercial magnetic board – try laying the chart on a cookie sheet, and holding it in place with a refrigerator magnet. Be sure to place the straightedge *above* your current working row, so you can compare it to the rows you have already knit.

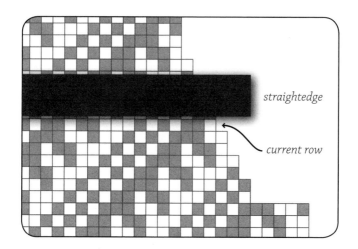

straightedge

current row

 *Anytime you copy a chart, please remember to respect the designer's copyright by keeping the copy with the original: if you sell or give away one, the other has to go with it or be destroyed.*

## Summary

❋ A chart for an entire garment piece can show both the shape of the piece and the patterning that fills that shape.

❋ Such charts are often quite large. To minimize clutter, symbols such as $\boxed{\text{Q}}$ and $\boxed{\text{K}}$ are often omitted in favor of letting outlines – perhaps for multiple sizes – show where to increase and decrease.

❋ To save space, just one half of a mirror-image chart might be printed.

❋ Safeguard your sanity by enlarging charts when necessary, and by using a straightedge to follow a given row.

With these exercises, test your ability to follow a chart that shows the shape of a knitted piece:

1. Examine this chart for a sleeve cap. Note that it specifies shaping through outlines only. If the chart didn't come with written shaping instructions, where would you shape via decreases? Where would you shape via bind-offs?

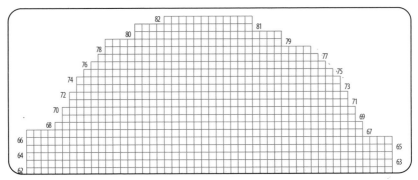

2. Cast on 3 stitches and knit a swatch, following this chart for the right-side rows and purling all the stitches on the wrong-side rows. Either follow the chart as it's shown here, or redraw it first to show both mirror-image halves.

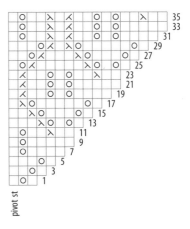

# Counting stitches

## Sometimes stitch counts vary

The number of stitches on your needles is often the same from row to row. But sometimes the stitch count varies in order to shape a piece. And sometimes it varies even within a single stitch pattern.

Clearly, your stitch count changes as a sleeve gets wider, or a mitten hand tapers to its tip. But your stitch count can vary even if a knitted piece remains the same width.

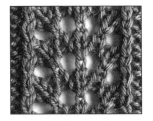

In lace, yarn overs might be matched by decreases not on the same row, but on some other row. These minor changes in stitch count disappear with blocking.

Increases at the base of a Celtic knot or some other "infinite" cable counteract the cable's tendency to compress fabric across its width. Decreases above the cable restore the original stitch count.

Textured knitting relies on a cluster of increases, followed by decreases on subsequent rows, to create nupps, embossed leaves, and other three-dimensional "poufs."

Even though their stitch counts vary, these stitch patterns remain the same width. Likewise, the charts for these stitch patterns remain the same width, with the same number of squares on each row.

## Counting chart squares can be misleading

Count the stitches shown by a chart, and you have figured out how many stitches should be on your needles at the end of a given row. Since each chart square typically matches one stitch, it's tempting to count chart squares. Yet that approach can be misleading.

Most of the time, each chart square matches one stitch on your needles, after you've completed that row. That's why k2tog and yo symbols, $\boxed{\diagup}$ and $\boxed{\text{O}}$, are both one square wide: even though k2tog "uses up" two stitches on your left needle and yo doesn't use any, both produce one stitch on your right needle. It's also why $\boxed{\diagdown\!\!\!\!\diagup}$ is four squares wide: working a two-over-two cable cross produces four stitches on your right needle.

So, to find out how many stitches should be on your needles at the end of a row, you would think you could just count chart squares. Here's the catch: some symbols flout the usual "one square matches one stitch on your right needle" rule.

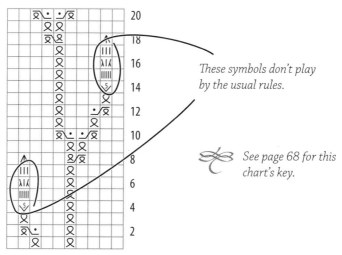

*These symbols don't play by the usual rules.*

See page 68 for this chart's key.

Flouting the usual rules lets a chart have straight edges – like the stitch pattern it represents – even though the stitch count changes from row to row. The number of chart squares is the same for each row, but the symbols within those squares might match more or fewer stitches. Counting stitches, then, becomes a matter of paying attention to chart **symbols** rather than chart **squares**.

The following pages describe symbols worthy of special mention.

## No-stitch symbols are placeholders
Phantoms. Ghosts of stitches that aren't there.

When a chart key labels a symbol as "no stitch," it means just that: the symbol doesn't match any stitches. A no-stitch symbol says, "Sure, there's a square here in the chart. But there isn't a corresponding stitch on your needles."

For example, row 1 of this lace chart has the most stitches, with four yarn overs but only two decreases. Row 3 has two decreases, but no yarn overs. As a result, it's two stitches narrower, as shown by the two no-stitch symbols.

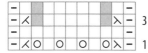

Reading across row 3, you would work p1, ssk, k5 (ignoring the squares with the no-stitch symbols), k2tog, p1.

In this example, the rows with the most stitches appear in the center of the cable chart.

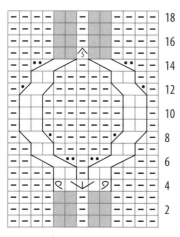

No-stitch symbols show that the first rows and the last rows contain four fewer stitches:

☀ Rows 1, 2, and 3 contain four fewer stitches because the increases on row 4 have not yet occured.

☀ Rows 15-18 contain four fewer stitches because of the decreases on row 15.

As per usual, reviewing a chart's key is worth a few moments of your time, since no-stitch symbols come in assorted flavors.

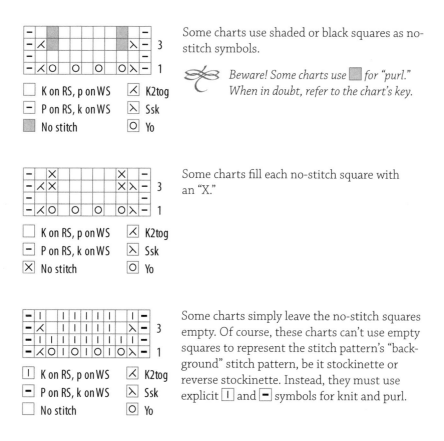

Some charts use shaded or black squares as no-stitch symbols.

✎ *Beware! Some charts use* ▨ *for "purl." When in doubt, refer to the chart's key.*

Some charts fill each no-stitch square with an "X."

Some charts simply leave the no-stitch squares empty. Of course, these charts can't use empty squares to represent the stitch pattern's "background" stitch pattern, be it stockinette or reverse stockinette. Instead, they must use explicit ⊡ and ⊟ symbols for knit and purl.

No matter what symbol a chart uses to say "no stitch," **just gloss over the symbol** as you read across a chart row. Remember, each no-stitch symbol is merely a placeholder on the chart, indicating a spot where an increase hasn't yet taken place or a decrease has taken place.

## Some symbols stand for more than one stitch

Though they're only one square wide, working one of these symbols results in multiple stitches on your right needle.

A no-stitch symbol flouts the "one square matches one stitch" rule by matching zero stitches. Other symbols take the opposite approach, matching more than one stitch.

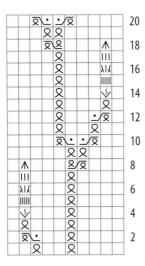

In this chart, each rosebud widens from a single stitch to five, then narrows to three before shrinking back to a single stitch. Yet the symbols for the rosebuds remain a single square wide, allowing the vines to flow uninterrupted through the rest of the chart.

☐ P1 on RS, k1 on WS ← *Note that an empty square means reverse stockinette! See page 16.*

Ⴒ K1 tbl on RS, p1 tbl on WS

·⁄Ⴒ Slip 1 st to cn and hold in back, k1 tbl, p1 from cn

Ⴒ·. Slip 1 st to cn and hold in front, p1, k1 tbl from cn

Ⴒ⁄Ⴒ Slip 1 st to cn and hold in back, k1 tbl, k1 tbl from cn

Ⴒ\Ⴒ Slip 1 st to cn and hold in front, k1 tbl, k1 tbl from cn

⋀ Sl2-k1-p2sso

║║ K3 on RS, p3 on WS

⋋⋌ K2tog, k1, ssk

║║║ K5 on RS, p5 on WS

ⱽ [K1, yo, k1, yo, k1] in next st

*Each of these four symbols results in more than one stitch on your right needle.*

A symbol that matches more than one stitch can make an effort to look like those stitches, squeezing the necessary notation into the confined space – for example, ⋏I⋌ instead of ⟨⋏ I ⋌⟩.

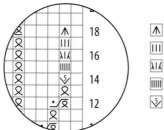

- Λ  Sl2-k1-p2sso
- III  K3 on RS, p3 on WS
- ⋏I⋌  K2tog, k1, ssk
- IIIII  K5 on RS, p5 on WS
- ⋎  [K1, yo, k1, yo, k1] in next st

Or a chart can opt for legibility over visual likeness, choosing arbitrary symbols such as (2).

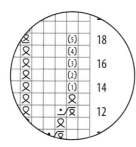

- (5)  Sl2-k1-p2sso
- (4)  K3 on RS, p3 on WS
- (3)  K2tog, k1, ssk
- (2)  K5 on RS, p5 on WS
- (1)  [K1, yo, k1, yo, k1] in next st

Or a chart can treat each embossed bud, leaf, or other "pouf" as a unit. Specially marked squares within the chart correspond to a separate, smaller chart drawn to the side. This auxiliary chart conveys both the dimensions of the pouf, and exactly how to work it.

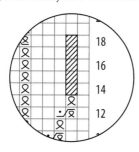
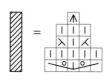

## Count the stitches produced by each symbol

Don't go by the number of squares, but by the meaning of the symbol in each square.

Let's say you've completed a row, and you're not sure you still have the right number of stitches on your needles. How do you figure it out?

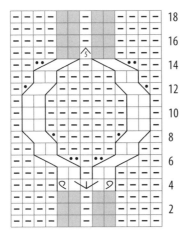

Reading across a chart row, add up the number of stitches produced on your right needle by working each symbol.

As you read each row of this chart, **ignore the no-stitch symbols**.

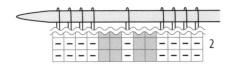

Read across row 2, counting the purls. The total is nine stitches.

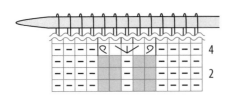

Now read across row 4. Four purls, a "make 1", a double increase that results in three stitches, another "make 1," and four more purls add up to thirteen stitches.

*Will you have gaps between the stitches on your needles, or stitches bunched tightly together? Of course not. The diagrams in this chapter show gaps and bunches only to let you see how the chart symbols correspond to stitches.*

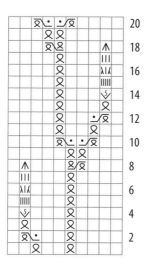

As you read each row of this chart, **pay extra attention to symbols that stand for multiple stitches**.

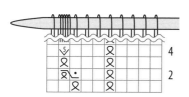

Consider row 4. A total of eight purls, one twisted knit, and a 🖳 increase that results in five stitches add up to a grand total of fourteen stitches.

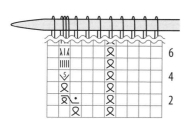

Turn to row 6. It also has eight purls and a twisted knit, but replaces 🖳 with 𝄗. This 𝄗 symbol means "k2tog, k1, ssk," so it results in three stitches. As a whole, working row 6 produces twelve stitches on your right needle.

## Count the stitches required by each symbol

Figure out how many stitches you'll need to work a chart row by adding up the number of stitches required to work each symbol in the row.

Imagine you have a pattern that tells you to work the following chart over nine stitches.

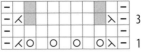

That doesn't seem quite right, does it? The chart is eleven squares wide. You can double-check the pattern by adding up the number of stitches required to work each symbol in row 1.

How many stitches do you need to follow a symbol's instructions? Well, that depends on what the symbol is telling you to do, *not* how wide the symbol is.

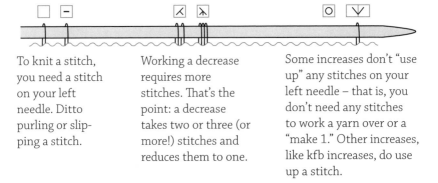

To knit a stitch, you need a stitch on your left needle. Ditto purling or slipping a stitch.

Working a decrease requires more stitches. That's the point: a decrease takes two or three (or more!) stitches and reduces them to one.

Some increases don't "use up" any stitches on your left needle – that is, you don't need any stitches to work a yarn over or a "make 1." Other increases, like kfb increases, do use up a stitch.

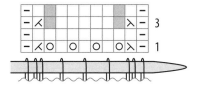

For row 1 of this chart, you'll need one stitch to work each knit and purl, two stitches for each decrease, but *no* stitches for the yarn overs, for a grand total of nine stitches – even though the chart is eleven squares wide.

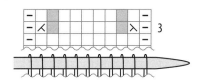

Row 2 requires eleven stitches, for simple knits and purls.

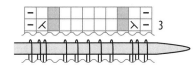

Row 3 also requires eleven stitches: one for each knit and purl, and two for each decrease. The no-stitch symbols, of course, do not count.

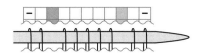

Finally, working row 4 requires just nine stitches: one for each of two purls, and one for each of seven knits.

No doubt, if you're following a pattern for a garment or accessory, it will tell you how many stitches to cast on, and over how many stitches to begin working each of its charts. But you can see how counting the stitches required to work a row lets you double-check pattern instructions like these. Really, it lets you determine how many stitches you should have on your left needle before beginning *any* row of a chart, not just the first row. And – as you'll soon see – it gives you a way of figuring out if a chart contains an error.

## Count stitches to suss out chart goofs

Sometimes, no matter how carefully you follow a chart, you wind up with the wrong number of stitches at the end of a row. How do you know if you've goofed, or if the chart contains a goof? (It does happen, on rare occasion!) Suss out errors of this sort by comparing stitch counts for adjacent rows.

Say you're nearing the end of row 9 on this edging pattern.

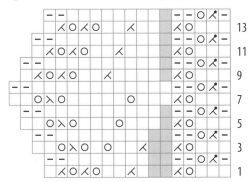

You're pretty sure you started the row with the correct number of stitches. After completing the last k2tog, the chart says you need to k1. But two stitches remain on your left needle. What do you do?

Your first step is to compare your knitting to the chart. Read along the chart row, comparing the symbols in the chart to the stitches on your right needle. Have you followed this row of the chart correctly to this point?

Yes: the symbols and stitches match. So why do two stitches remain on your left needle?

If you have followed the chart faithfully to this point, it's possible the chart is in error. Maybe an increase or decrease symbol is misplaced. Or maybe a row has the wrong number of squares or no-stitch symbols.

You can confirm that a chart contains an error by comparing two stitch counts:

❊ the stitches *produced* by working a row, as described on page 70, and

❊ the stitches *required* to work the following row, as described on page 72.

These stitch counts ought to match. If they don't, the chart has a goof.

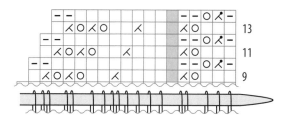

*Row 9 requires eighteen stitches.*

*Yet row 8 produces nineteen stitches*
*– something is wrong!*

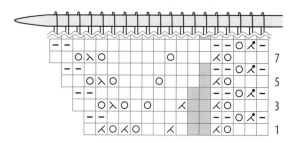

Just knowing that the chart is wrong – knowing that you haven't goofed, and that you're not imagining things – can be a relief. It's your signal to put your knitting aside while you:

❊ compare the chart to accompanying written instructions (if it has any);

❊ check for errata on the publisher's website; or

❊ make an educated guess, draw a revised chart, and knit a test swatch from the revised chart.

And the problem with this chart? Its written instructions or errata ought to reveal that the culprit is the 人 in the middle of row 9. It should be a 人.

## Summary

☀ Charts show changes in stitch count not just by matching the shape of the knitted fabric, with more chart squares on wider rows. They also use special symbols: no-stitch symbols that act as placeholders, and symbols that squeeze more than one stitch into a single chart square.

☀ The key to being able to count the stitches shown by a chart is to consider the symbols within the chart squares.

☀ Counting the stitches produced by working a row, and the stitches required to work a row, lets you know how many stitches should be on your needles. Comparing the stitch counts for adjacent rows lets you know if the chart is legit or if it contains a goof.

Test your ability to count stitches with these exercises:

1. How many stitches are required to work each row of this chart?

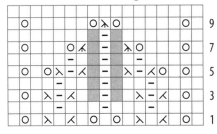

2. Does this chart contain a goof? If so, on which row(s)?

# Repeated stitches

## Charts highlight repeated stitches in many ways

Brackets, boxes, lines, or shading: one way or another, a chart distinguishes between stitches that are repeated, and edge stitches that fall outside the repeat.

Many stitch patterns have a "repeat," a group of stitches that gets repeated across a row. Written instructions highlight repeated stitches with * or []. Charts highlight them visually – for example, each of the charts below marks the same repeated stitches in its own way.

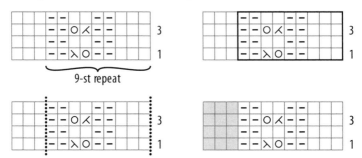

Stitches that aren't repeated fall outside the highlighted area. In written instructions, these edge stitches may appear before, after, or both before and after the * or [] that surround the repeated stitches. In charts, the edge stitches may be to the left, to the right, or both to the left and to the right of the repeated stitches. For example, in the charts above, the edge stitches appear to the left of the repeated stitches. In the chart below, they appear on both sides of the chart.

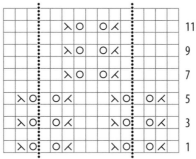

 *Will the placement of a chart's repeat lines match the * or [] of accompanying written instructions? Not necessarily: to make the chart clear and the written instructions succinct, a row's repeat may differ between the two.*

## Repeat the highlighted stitches only

You'll create the bulk of a knitted fabric by working a chart's repeated stitches many times. But its edge stitches? You'll work them at most once per row.

When working flat, read the right-side rows from right to left and the wrong-side rows from left to right, as usual. On each row, work the highlighted stitches multiple times, but the edge stitches just once.

This chart highlights its repeated stitches by surrounding them with dotted lines. Since they appear on the right side of the chart, on right-side rows you'll work the repeated stitches multiple times, then work the edge stitches.

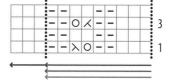

On wrong-side rows, you'll work the edge stitches first, then work the repeated stitches.

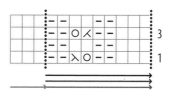

Following the chart in this way is like pretending someone had rubber-stamped copies of the chart's repeated section, laying them side by side as in the finished fabric.

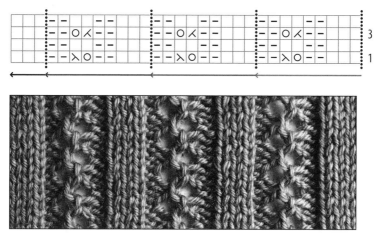

## Omit the edge stitches when they're not necessary

A stitch pattern's edge stitches aren't needed when the patterning has no edges – namely, when the patterning goes all the way around a piece.

Say you're knitting a sock in the round, following a chart for the patterning. On the foot, the patterning extends only across the top of the foot. On the leg, it extends all the way around the sock. Does this affect how you follow the chart?

You bet it does. Across the top of the foot, work the repeated stitches as many times as necessary, and the edge stitches just once, *just as when working flat.*

When following this chart
*over a portion of a round,*

☀ work the four stitches at the right edge once,

☀ work the eight stitches in the center repeatedly, then

☀ work the three stitches at the left edge once.

The edge stitches "balance" the stitch pattern, allowing the left and right edges to match.

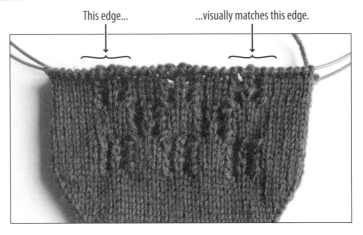

This edge... ...visually matches this edge.

 *Omit the edge stitches when working continuously in the round, such as around the leg of a sock.*

But when forming continuous patterning all the way around the sock's leg, *skip the edge stitches*. Simply repeat the highlighted stitches.

When following this chart *over an entire round*, just repeat the eight stitches in the center.

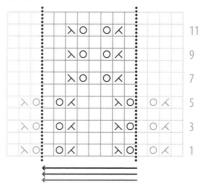

Omitting the edge stitches lets the pattern flow across the beginning of rounds.

Without edge stitches, the pattern is seamless, even at the beginning of rounds.

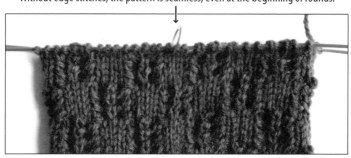

Essentially, when working a chart continuously around a piece, the chart's **right** repeat line marks the **beginning** of each round. Its **left** repeat line marks the **end** of each round.

## Sometimes repeat lines run through wide symbols
Relax. You don't have to figure out how to work half a symbol.

Have a look at row 8. At first glance, a knitter might wonder, "How am I supposed to follow this row? Before repeating the stitches between the dotted lines, how do I work the five edge stitches? Three are purled, but the other two are part of a cable cross. How do I work half a cable cross?"

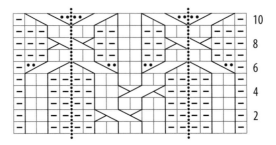

The answer: you don't. Have a closer look at row 8. The two dotted lines *each* run through the *same* cable cross symbol. The trick is to treat row 8 as if the repeat lines zig-zagged around *both* of the symbols.

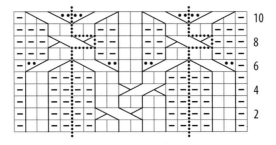

What does it mean when repeat lines zig-zag? Read on!

 *If one of a chart's repeat lines runs through a cable symbol, its other repeat line will always run through an identical cable symbol.*

## Sometimes repeat lines zig-zag

No matter: on each row, just repeat the stitches between the lines, wherever they may be.

---

Around wide symbols (like the cable crosses on the previous page), around motifs, or to match the * or [ ] of written instructions – for whatever reason, repeat lines sometimes zig-zag through a chart.

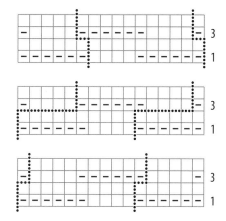

Even with the differences in their repeat lines, these charts all say essentially the same thing. Following them all results in the same knitted fabric.

Following these charts is the same as following charts with straight repeat lines, if you're working flat or if you're working a panel in the round.

On each row, just work the edge stitches before the first repeat line, repeat the stitches between the lines, then work the edge stitches after the second repeat line – wherever the lines may be on that row.

*Repeat these stitches when working rows 3 and 4.*

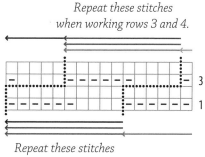

*Repeat these stitches when working rows 1 and 2.*

So zig-zag repeat lines don't really affect the way you follow a chart – *unless* you're repeating a stitch pattern continuously around a piece. The following pages explain what to do in that situation.

## Shift the beginning of rounds to match zig-zags

End the previous round a few stitches early to shift to the right, or work a few more stitches at the end of the previous round to shift to the left.

How would you follow this chart continuously around a piece?

Notice that the repeat lines zig-zag.

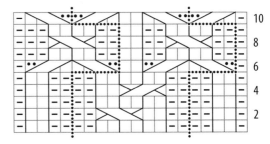

Remember to omit the edge stitches.

Looks a bit odd, doesn't it?

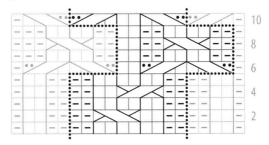

Remember also that a chart's right repeat line marks the beginning of each round. So, this chart shows that **your beginning-of-rounds marker has to shift.**

Before round 6, the marker has to shift four stitches to the right.

Before round 10, the marker has to shift four stitches to the left.

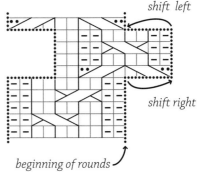

*shift left*

*shift right*

*beginning of rounds*

Specifically, here's what you would do:

☀ To start round 6 four stitches to the right of round 5, **end round 5 four stitches early.**

Work the last repeat as
☐☐☐☐ ─ ─ , then place a
new beginning-of-rounds
marker. Remove the old
marker when you come
to it.

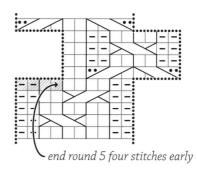

*end round 5 four stitches early*

☀ To start round 10 four stitches to the left of round 9, **complete round 9 and work four more stitches.**

*complete round 9, then work four more stitches*

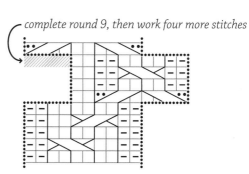

Come to the end of round
9, remove the beginning-
of-rounds marker, work
four more stitches, then
replace the beginning-of-
rounds marker.

How should those four extra stitches be worked? In a word: inconspicuously. Knit the knit stitches and purl the purl stitches to maintain the patterning of the previous row.

## Shift to keep lace decreases aligned

When working lace, you sometimes need to shift the beginning of rounds by a stitch or two before working a decrease. Your pattern ought to tell you when this is necessary.

Sometimes, when working lace, stitches that sit on both sides of the beginning-of-rounds marker need to be worked together in a decrease. Before working the decrease, you have to shift the beginning-of-rounds marker out of the way. Or, if you prefer, you can think of this as moving a stitch across the beginning of rounds.

In this example, the stitch before the beginning-of-rounds marker and the two stitches after the marker need to be decreased together at the beginning of the next round. But first, the marker needs to be shifted out of the way, to the right. Stated differently, the stitch on the right needs to move left across the beginning of rounds.

In this example, the stitches on each side of the beginning-of-rounds marker need to be decreased together at the end of this round. But first, the marker needs to be shifted out of the way, to the left. Looking at it from another perspective, the stitch on the left needs to move to the right across the beginning of rounds.

Either way, your pattern should tell you what to do. Usually, arrows at the chart's right edge show in which direction stitches should move. Here are a couple examples:

At the beginning of round 7, **move a stitch from right to left** across the beginning of rounds:

❋ End round 6 one stitch early.

❋ Slip that last stitch to your right needle.

❋ Remove the beginning-of-rounds marker.

❋ Slip the stitch back to your left needle.

❋ Replace the marker.

This shifts the beginning-of-rounds marker one stitch to the right. Now you're ready to work the first decrease.

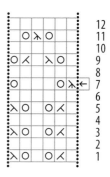

For this chart, **move a stitch from left to right** across the beginning of round 9:

❋ Complete round 8.

❋ Remove the beginning-of-rounds marker.

❋ Slip the next stitch (or work it inconspicuously, in pattern).

❋ Replace the marker.

This shifts the beginning-of-rounds marker one stitch to the left so that, at the end of round 9, you'll have all the stitches you need to complete the last decrease.

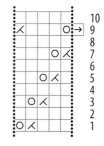

 *Did you notice that every row of these two charts is numbered on the right? That says the charts are geared only for use in the round. They don't include the edge stitches you would need when working flat.*

# Trust your knitting

Sometimes the repeat lines of a chart can lead you astray. Then, to keep the parts of a stitch pattern aligned correctly, you have to rely on your ability to read your knitting and think for yourself.

Some charts are a snap to repeat around a piece. Others show – via zig-zag repeat lines, arrows, or some other notation – that you need to shift your beginning-of-rounds marker on some rounds.

A few charts, unfortunately, can be misleading.

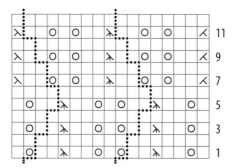

With its zig-zag repeat lines, you would think this chart is telling you to shift your marker at the beginning of every other round. Not true: the repeat lines just show the zig-zag path your marker will take automatically, as yarn overs nudge it one way and decreases pull it the other.

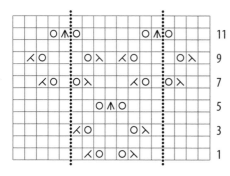

With its straight repeat lines, you would think this chart is telling you that your beginning-of-rounds marker can stay put. But if the chart had been drawn specifically for use in the round, it would include a symbol instructing you to shift the marker at the beginning of round 11, before the Λ.

What's a knitter to do, when repeat lines can be misleading?

Trust your knitting. And rely on your own judgement. Remember one of the great joys of charts is that they're pictures of knitted fabric. As you begin each round, ask yourself: are the yarn overs, decreases, and other stitches in your knitting lining up like the symbols of the chart? If not, unknit to back up, and shift the beginning of rounds so the stitches do line up.

Consider these samples, which are being knit according to the charts on the facing page.

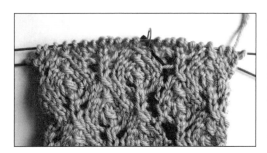

You can see that this sample matches the top chart. Its yarn overs and decreases align as in the chart, despite the zig-zag path of the beginning-of-rounds marker (shown here by the contrast-color waste yarn).

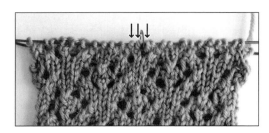

To center the ⚠ double decrease at the beginning of round 11 above the yarn overs of the previous rounds, it's clear that a stitch before and two stitches after the marker need to be decreased together.

## Summary

❀ Regardless of how a chart highlights its repeated stitches, work those stitches over and over to create the majority of the fabric.

❀ Work the edge stitches just once per row, if working flat or if working a panel in the round.

❀ Omit the edge stitches if working continuously in the round, and remember that the right repeat line marks the beginning of each round.

❀ Shift your beginning-of-rounds marker if the repeat lines zig-zag, if instructed by chart symbols, or as necessary to keep your stitches lined up like the symbols of the chart.

With these exercises, test your ability to manage charts with repeated stitches:

1. Have a look at this chart. How many stitches would you need to cast on, if you wanted to knit a flat swatch consisting of three repeats of the pattern plus its edge stitches? How many would you need to cast on to work five repeats in the round?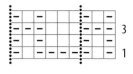

2. Knit a flat swatch, according to the above chart or any other chart in this chapter (except those on page 87, which aren't meant for knitting flat). Be sure to cast on enough stitches for three repeats of the pattern plus its edge stitches. Notice how the edge stitches "balance" the pattern.

3. Knit an in-the-round swatch according to the same chart, casting on enough stitches for five repeats (or more repeats, if you prefer larger rounds). Check that the pattern runs seamlessly around the swatch.

4. Knit an in-the-round swatch according to one of the charts on page 87. Work through all the rounds of the chart a few times, shifting your beginning-of-rounds marker as indicated. Check that the pattern runs seamlessly from the bottom of your swatch to its top.

# Answers to selected exercises

Deepen your understanding of charts: work through the exercises at the end of each chapter, *then* check your work below.

### The Big Picture, page 22

1. Match each of these charts to its swatch photo.

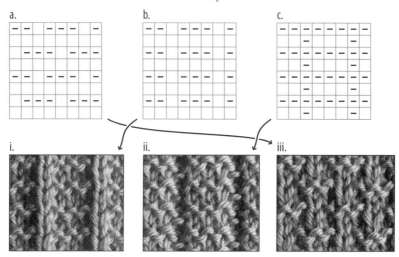

*Chart a and photo iii both show groups of purls staggered like bricks. Chart b and photo i show garter stitch broken by knit columns, while chart c and photo ii show garter stitch broken by purl columns.*

# Staying on track, page 32

1. Of the following statements, which are accurate descriptions of the chart shown here? Which are false?

   a. A panel of stockinette-based lace, 6 stitches wide, is flanked by columns of purl stitches. *True.*

   b. Lace patterning takes place on every right-side row. *False. Rows 1 and 9 do not have any lace patterning.*

   c. In the lower half of the chart, a line of three yarn overs runs diagonally from the lower right to the upper left. Matching k2tog form a line to the left of the yarn overs. *False. The decreases are ssk, not k2tog.*

   d. In the upper half of the chart, yarn overs and k2tog run diagonally from the lower left to the upper right. *True.*

   | | | | | | | | | |
   |---|---|---|---|---|---|---|---|---|
   | – | | | | | | | – | |
   | – | | | O | | | ⟋ | – | 15 |
   | – | | | | | | | – | |
   | – | | O | | | ⟋ | | – | 13 |
   | – | | | | | | | – | |
   | – | O | | | ⟋ | | | – | 11 |
   | – | | | | | | | – | |
   | – | | | | | | | – | 9 |
   | – | | | | | | | – | |
   | – | ⟍ | | | O | | | – | 7 |
   | – | | | | | | | – | |
   | – | | ⟍ | | | O | | – | 5 |
   | – | | | | | | | – | |
   | – | | | ⟍ | | | O | – | 3 |
   | – | | | | | | | – | |
   | – | | | | | | | – | 1 |

2. This sample is being knit according the chart shown above. Which row is currently being knit? How can you tell?

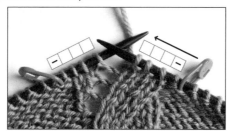

*The stitches on the right needle were worked most recently, as part of a right-side row, so the knitter is in the middle of a right-side row. The ⬚⬚⬚– sequence appears at the start of right-side rows 1 and 9, so the knitter is in the middle of row 1 or 9. The right-slanting line of yarn overs appears on rows 11–15 of the chart, so the knitter must be in the middle of the following right-side row, which is row 1.*

## Cable symbol sensibility, page 48

1. For these crosses, is the cable needle held in front or in back?

    a. ☑️ *Back (for most knitters – lefty knitters, hold to front)*

    b. ⊤▪⊤⊥ *Front (for most knitters – lefty knitters, hold to back)*

    c. ⊳⊱⊰⊲ *Front (for most knitters – lefty knitters, hold to back)*

2. Match each of these symbols to its definition.

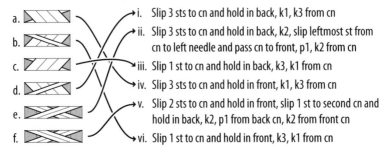

    a.

    b.

    c.

    d.

    e.

    f.

    i.   Slip 3 sts to cn and hold in back, k1, k3 from cn

    ii.  Slip 3 sts to cn and hold in back, k2, slip leftmost st from cn to left needle and pass cn to front, p1, k2 from cn

    iii. Slip 1 st to cn and hold in back, k3, k1 from cn

    iv.  Slip 3 sts to cn and hold in front, k1, k3 from cn

    v.   Slip 2 sts to cn and hold in front, slip 1 st to second cn and hold in back, k2, p1 from back cn, k2 from front cn

    vi.  Slip 1 st to cn and hold in front, k3, k1 from cn

## Charts that show shape, page 62

1. Examine this chart for a sleeve cap. Note that it specifies shaping through outlines only. If the chart didn't come with written shaping instructions, where would you shape via decreases? Where would you shape via bind-offs?

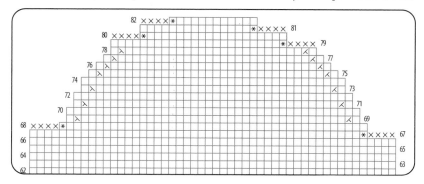

*This chart shows one possible solution. Bind-offs are used when the outline shows more than a single stitch has been lost at the beginning of a row. Decreases are placed one stitch in from the edge, leaving a plain selvedge stitch for seaming. The decreases lean "outwards," creating subtle decrease lines. Other solutions are possible too – for example, placing ssk at the right edge of the sleeve cap and k2tog at the left edge would cause the decreases to lean "inwards" and create prominent decrease lines.*

2. Cast on 3 stitches and knit a swatch, following this chart for the right-side rows and purling all the stitches on the wrong-side rows. Either follow the chart as it's shown here, or redraw it first to show both mirror-image halves.

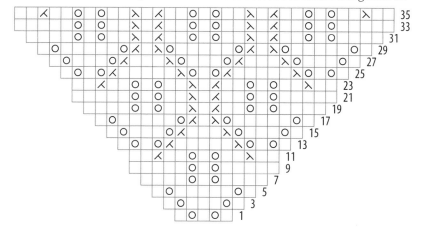

1. How many stitches are required to work each row of this chart?

| | | | | | | | | | | |
|---|---|---|---|---|---|---|---|---|---|---|
| − | ⅋ | − | | | ⅄ | | | − | ⅋ | − |
| − | ⅋ | − | | ⅄ | | ⅄ | | − | ⅋ | − |
| − | ⅋ | − | | − | | − | | − | ⅋ | − |
| − | ⅋ | O | | O | | O | | O | ⅋ | − |

9 stitches
11 stitches    3
11 stitches
7 stitches    1

2. Does this chart contain a goof? *No. The number of stitches produced by working each row of the chart matches the number of stitches required to work the following row.*

| | | | | | | | | | | | | |
|---|---|---|---|---|---|---|---|---|---|---|---|---|
| O | | | | O | ⅄ | O | | | | O | | 9 |
| | | | | | − | | | | | | | |
| O | | | O | ⅄ | − | | ⅄ | O | | O | | 7 |
| | | − | | − | | − | | | | | | |
| O | O | ⅄ | − | ⅄ | − | ⅄ | − | ⅄ | O | O | | 5 |
| | − | | | − | | − | | | | | | |
| O | ⅄ | − | ⅄ | | − | | ⅄ | − | ⅄ | O | | 3 |
| | − | | | − | | − | | | | | | |
| O | ⅄ | | ⅄ | O | | O | ⅄ | | ⅄ | O | | 1 |

### Repeated stitches, page 90

1. Have a look at this chart. How many stitches would you need to cast on, if you wanted to knit a flat swatch consisting of three repeats of the pattern plus its edge stitches? *Twenty-one: three repeats of 6 stitches is 18 stitches, plus 3 edge stitches totals 21 stitches.*

How many would you need to cast on to work five repeats in the round? *Thirty: five repeats of 6 stitches (without any edge stitches) is 30 stitches.*

# Key to charts and list of abbreviations

This key lists all the symbols commonly used within this book. Additional symbols, used for comparison purposes or to explain a particular point, are described near the charts in which they appear.

## Basic symbols

☐ Knit on RS, purl on WS, *unless directed otherwise*

Ⅰ Knit on RS, purl on WS

− Purl on RS, knit on WS

Ⴥ K1 tbl on RS, p1 tbl on WS

## Increases

Ο Yo

ℜ M1L

⅁ M1R

⋁ Kfb

⋎ Ctr dbl inc

## Decreases

⋋ K2tog on RS, p2tog on WS

⋌ P2tog on RS, k2tog on WS

⋊ Ssk on RS, ssp on WS

⋌ K3tog on RS, p3tog on WS

⋋ Sl1-k2tog-psso

⋀ Sl2-k1-p2sso

⤳ 5-to-1 dec

## Miscellaneous symbols

→ Move 1 st from left to right across the beginning of rounds; see page 87

← Move 1 st from right to left across the beginning of rounds; see page 87

⊠ Cast on

✕ Bind off

∗ Indicates st remaining on right needle at completion of bind-off; see page 53

↻ W&t to WS

↺ W&t to RS

▨ No stitch; see page 66

## Cable crosses

Slip 1 st to cn and hold in front, k1, k1 from cn

Slip 1 st to cn and hold in back, k2, p1 from cn

Slip 2 sts to cn and hold in front, p1, k2 from cn

Slip 2 sts to cn and hold in back, k2, k2 from cn

Slip 2 sts to cn and hold in front, k2, k2 from cn

Slip 2 sts to cn and hold in back, k2, p2 from cn

Slip 2 sts to cn and hold in front, p2, k2 from cn

Slip 4 sts to cn and hold in back, k2, slip leftmost 2 sts from cn to left needle and pass cn to front, k2, k2 from cn

Slip 2 sts to cn and hold in front, slip 2 sts to second cn and hold in back, k2, k2 from back cn, k2 from front cn

| | |
|---|---|
| **5-to-1 dec** | Slip 3 sts to right needle, *pass second st on right needle over first st and off right needle, slip 1 st to left needle, pass second st on left needle over first st and off left needle*, slip 1 st to right needle, repeat from * to * once, k1. |
| **cn** | Cable needle. |
| **ctr dbl inc** (center double increase) | [K1 tbl, k1] in next st, insert left needle from left to right under vertical strand between sts just made, knit this strand tbl. |
| **k** | Knit. |
| **k2tog** | Knit 2 together. |
| **k3tog** | Knit 3 together. |
| **kfb** | Knit into front and back of next st. |
| **M1L** (make 1 left) | Insert left needle from front to back under strand between needles, and knit into the back of this loop. |
| **M1R** (make 1 right) | Insert left needle from back to front under strand between needles, and knit into the front of this loop. |
| **p** | Purl. |
| **p2tog** | Purl 2 together. |
| **p3tog** | Purl 3 together. |
| **RS** | Right side. |
| **sl1-k2tog-psso** | Slip a st knitwise, k2tog, pass slipped st over k2tog. |
| **sl2-k1-p2sso** | Slip 2 sts as if to k2tog, k1, pass 2 slipped sts over knit st. |
| **ssk** (slip, slip, knit) | [Slip a st knitwise] twice. Insert left needle from left to right into fronts of both sts, and knit together through back loops. |
| **ssp** (slip, slip, purl) | [Slip a st knitwise] twice. Slip both sts back to left needle. Purl together through back loops by inserting right needle from left to right into backs of both sts. |
| **st(s)** | Stitch(es). |
| **tbl** | Through back loop. |
| **w&t** (wrap and turn) | Slip next st to right needle, bring yarn between needle tips, slip st back to left needle, turn. |
| **WS** | Wrong side. |
| **yo** | Yarn over. |

# Index

See the first page of each chapter for a list of its topics, or the last page of each chapter for a summary of its main points.

# Acknowledgments

For years, I've read the acknowledgments sections of other authors' books. Each seemed to begin with, "This book would not have been possible without the help of many people." Now I know what those authors were talking about.

Thanks go to the authors of the plethora of knitting books on my shelves, for showing all of us the marvelous directions that charts can take us. Barbara Walker's classic, *Charted Knitting Designs*, deserves special mention. As best I know, it was the first book to tout the benefits of charts – and it has done so, to countless knitters, for decades.

Thanks go to the students in my classes, who continually show me how a handful of key concepts can unlock a world of chart-based knitting. Your enthusiasm keeps my appreciation of charts fresh and alive.

Thanks go to Donna Druchunas. Though she doesn't know it, her innocent observation that I seem to prefer short-term projects spurred me to tackle at least one long-term project – this book – to prove to myself that I could see it through.

Thanks go to Janet Szabo, for sparking the drive to self-publish. My mind boggles at the thought of all the inane questions you've patiently answered over the years.

Thanks go to Cat Bordhi and the other Visionaries, for sharing nuts-and-bolts publishing information and much-needed reality checks within the cocoon of a supportive community. Let's all look forward to the day when yarn shops can display an entire shelf of Visionary books, each true to its own vision.

Special thanks go to Grace Jarvis, Marcie Ruskin, Lorilee Beltman, Joan Schrouder, Mark Irons, Deb Robson, and Cat Bordhi, for graciously taking the time to review and comment on early drafts of this book, and to my tech editor, Karen Frisa, who diligently brought to my attention the numerous warts and blemishes I had been refusing to see. You should all know I appreciate your efforts, even if I stubbornly insisted on using questionable words like "dime-store" and "colorize."

Thanks also to Dave, for his unconditional support. This book's for you, sweetie pie.